Minutes a Day-Mastery for a Lifetime!

level 3

English Grammar
& Writing Mechanics

Nancy McGraw & Nancy Tondy

Bright Ideas Press, LLC
Cleveland, Ohio

Summer Solutions Level 3
English Grammar & Writing Mechanics

All rights reserved. No part of this publication may be reproduced or transmitted in any form or by any means, electronic or mechanical, including photocopy, recording, or any information storage or retrieval system. Reproduction of these materials for an entire class, school, or district is prohibited.

Printed in the United States of America

ISBN 13: 978-1-934210-04-8
ISBN 10: 1-934210-04-8

Cover Design: Dan Mazzola
Editor: Kimberly A. Dambrogio

Copyright © 2008 by Bright Ideas Press, LLC
Cleveland, Ohio

Instructions for Parents/Guardians

- *Summer Solutions* is an extension of the *Simple Solutions* Approach being used by thousands of children in schools across the United States.

- The 30 lessons included in each workbook are meant to review and reinforce the skills learned in the grade level just completed.

- The program is designed to be used three days per week for ten weeks to ensure retention.

- Completing the book all at one time defeats the purpose of sustained practice over the summer break.

- Each book contains answers for each lesson.

- Each book also contains the *Help Pages* which list vocabulary, parts of speech, editing marks, and rules for capitalization, punctuation, and spelling.

- Lessons should be checked immediately for optimal feedback.

- Adjust the use of the book to fit vacations. More lessons may have to be completed during the weeks before or following a family vacation.

Summer Solutions Level 3
English Grammar & Writing Mechanics

Reviewed Skills include:

- Sentences / Subject / Predicate
- Punctuation / Capitalization
- Spelling Rules
- Editing Marks / Sentence Writing
- Compound Words
- Common and Proper Nouns
- Pronouns
- Verbs / Present, Past, Future / Irregular Verbs
- Adjectives
- Adverbs
- Synonyms / Antonyms / Homophones
- Plurals / Possessives
- Contractions
- Commas / Quotation Marks

Help Pages begin on page 63.
Answers to Lessons begin on page 69.

Lesson #1

1. Underline the correct past tense verb.

   Jeffrey has (grew / grown) four inches.

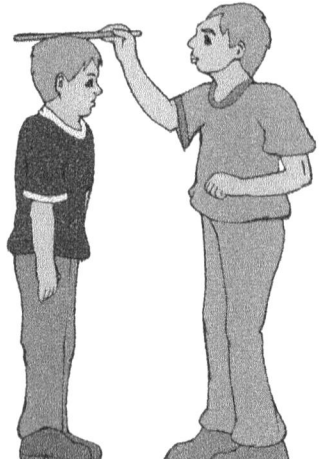

2. Underline the antonyms.

   heavy   fresh   funny   light

3. Underline the verb.

   The car crashed into the tree.

4. Drop the -e before adding -ing.

   arrive + -ing ➡ _____

   save + -ing ➡ _____

5. Every sentence begins with a _____ letter.

   capital   lower case

6. Write this sentence correctly.

   My family is ~~g~~/oing to ~~b~~razil in ~~j~~une⊙

   _____

   _____

7. Underline the correct verb.

   Tina has (did / done) all of her chores.

8. Circle the adjective that describes the underlined noun.

   The squirrel carried a huge <u>acorn</u>.

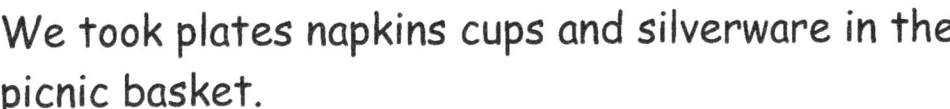

9. Insert the commas in this series.

   We took plates napkins cups and silverware in the picnic basket.

10. Write this name correctly.   dr. mason

    _____

Summer Solutions© Grammar & Writing   Level 3

Lesson #2

1. Which words can be used with *house* to make a compound word?

    fire   big   farm   pretty

2. Underline the subject.

    A lion tamer has a scary job.

3. Put quotation marks around what someone says.

    Janice said, I'm getting a new puppy today.

4. Circle a synonym for *enormous*.

    tiny   quick   huge   special

5. Choose the best word to complete the sentence.

    Sarah felt so _____ after she moved.

    likely   lonely   lovely

6. Choose the correct adjective.

   It stays lighter (longer / longest) during the summer.

7. Circle the correct pronoun.

   My father took Brad and (I / me) to the movies.

8. Use the editing marks for "add something" and "end punctuation" to improve this sentence.

   We saw many different kinds of monkeys at zoo

9. Which word will you join with *re-* to complete the sentence?

   Re_____ the song so I can hear the words.

   fill   heat   play   build

10. Underline the adjectives that tell *how many*.

    I have four brothers and two sisters.

Lesson #3

1. Cross out any misspelled words and write them correctly.

   going   night   swimer   happiest

   _____

2. Write the contractions.

   you are ➡ _____   was not ➡ _____

3. Use the editing marks for "capital letter" and "take something out" to correct this sentence.

   Maybe i will be in the your class next year.

4. Underline the adjective that compares.

   Firefighters are the bravest people I know.

5. Write a possessive pronoun (my, your, his, her, its, our, or their) to replace the underlined words.

   <u>The birds'</u> nest is on our porch. The nest is _____ home.

6. Write the plurals of these words.

   bush   church   stick

   _____   _____   _____

7. Add a comma and quotation marks.

   The nurse asked Do you have a cough?

8. Underline the article that should come before each word.

   (a / an) funny trick   (an / the) olive   (the / a) kittens

9. Circle the subject pronoun and underline the predicate.

   She bakes the most delicious cakes.

10. Use two editing marks to fix these sentences.

    We live on a fram. we have cows, sheep, and chickens.

Lesson #4

1. Add -*est* and -*er* to the word *warm* to make adjectives that compare.

   It is _____ in Hawaii than in Ohio.

   The _____ place in our house next to the fireplace.

2. Underline the adverb that tells how.

   The honeybee flew slowly from one flower to the next.

3. Write the correct abbreviation for each month of the year.

   | Apr.   Feb.   Dec. |

   _____ ➡ February

   _____ ➡ April

   _____ ➡ December

4 – 5. Sort these words into nouns and verbs.

   baby   trot   pony   bank   laugh   spell   pen

   Nouns: _____

   Verbs: _____

6 – 7. Write two sentences. Use one word from each list in items 4 – 5.

_____

_____

_____

_____

8. Write the past tense of *know*. _____

9. Write a possessive pronoun that agrees with the underlined nouns.

<u>Lynn and Marsha</u> put _____ coats on the hook.

10. Use the editing mark to show which words should begin with a capital letter.

pete does not have a game on saturday.

Lesson #5

1. Add a comma and quotation marks.

   Carter asked Why don't we have school tomorrow?

2. Underline two antonyms.

   simple   unusual   special   difficult

3. Underline the verb.

   Mike stirred the paint in the can.

4. Underline the proper nouns.

   Texas   church   Lake Erie   grocery

5. Underline the <u>subject</u> of the sentence.

   The sea otter has the thickest fur in the animal kingdom.

6. Use the mark for "add something" and "end punctuation" to fix this sentence.

   I like to eat fries with hamburger

7. Rewrite the sentence in #6 correctly.

   _____

8. Write the 2 words that make up each contraction.

   haven't ➡ _____ _____

   can't ➡ _____ _____

   isn't ➡ _____ _____

9. Underline the plural possessive noun.

   Jerry's cabin is next to the

   Wilsons' beach house.

10. Draw a line through the fragment. Add some words to the fragment and write it as a complete sentence on the line below.

    The billy goat ate everything in our garden. Even the

    flowers. It's favorite thing to eat is tomatoes.

    _____

Lesson #6

1. Use the prefix *un-* to write the opposite of these words.

   zip ➡ _____

   buckle ➡ _____

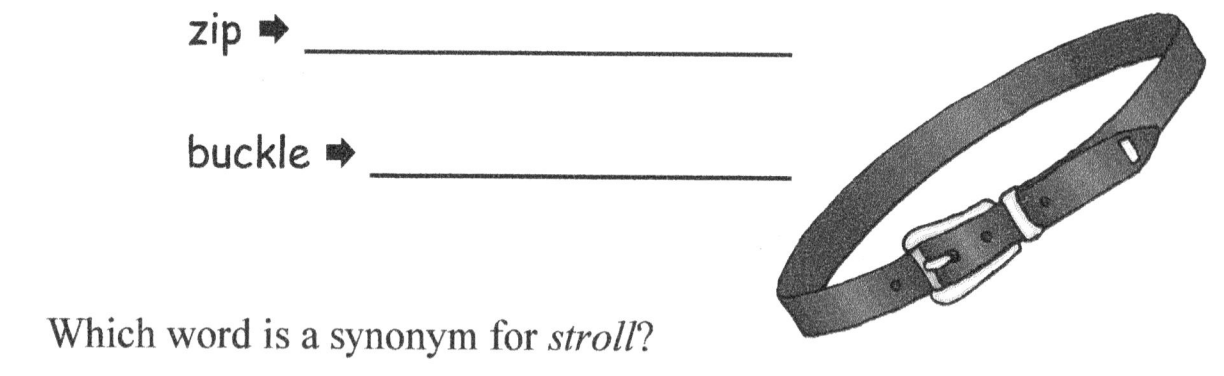

2. Which word is a synonym for *stroll*?

   race   crawl   walk   drive

3. Underline the adverb that tells *how*.

   The girl suddenly jumped up from her seat.

4. Insert an article to complete the sentence.

   We were walking, and _____ stray dog followed us home.

5. Underline the comparative (adjective that compares) in this sentence.

   Mercury is the closest planet to the sun.

Summer Solutions© Grammar & Writing   Level 3

6. Circle the adjectives that tell *how many*.

   Chad bought six books and two magazines at the Book Fair.

7. Match these abbreviations with the months of the year.

   Feb.   Nov.   Dec.

   _____ ➡ November

   _____ ➡ February

   _____ ➡ December

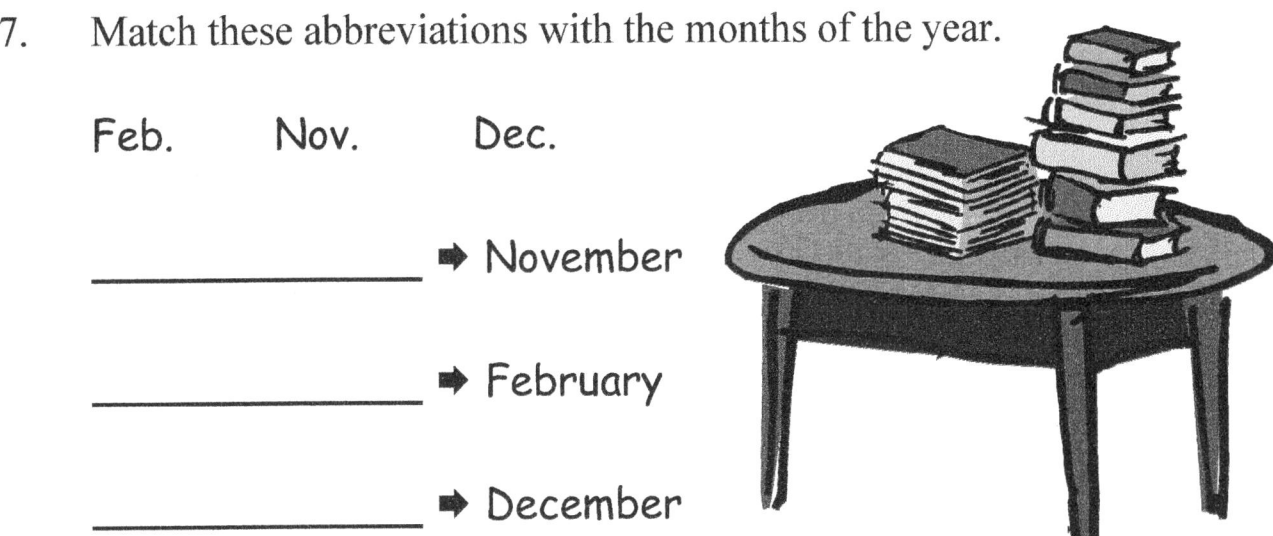

8. Add a comma and quotation marks to fix this sentence.

   Mrs. Gomez said Your project is due on Tuesday.

9. Use two editing marks to fix this sentence.

   In which month valentine's Day?

10. Rewrite the sentence above correctly.

Lesson #7

1. Underline the proper nouns in this sentence.

   Hawaii is part of the United States.

2. Underline the subject of the sentence.

   Grandma took me to my piano lesson.

3. Underline the <u>singular possessive</u> noun.

   Our neighbor's barn caught on fire.

4. Which verb shows <u>present tense</u>?

   rode   took   ran   will speak   shows

5. An adverb describes a verb. Circle the adverb.

   We carefully dried the dishes.

Summer Solutions© Grammar & Writing   Level 3

6. Write the abbreviation for *Wednesday*. _____

7. What is the meaning of *meatless*?

   _____

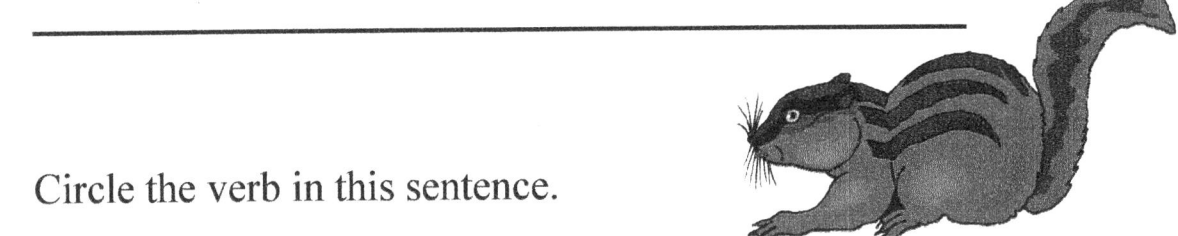

8. Circle the verb in this sentence.

   The chipmunk hid under a pile of leaves.

9 – 10. Brainstorm some things that computers help you do.

15

Lesson #8

1. An adverb describes a verb. Underline the adverb.

    The car raced noisily down the street.

2. **Adverbs can tell *when* and *where* an action takes place. Sort these adverbs into two lists.**

    today   next   soon   away   around   near   often

    When: _____

    Where: _____

3. Underline the correct helping verb.

    The children (has / have) eaten lunch already.

4. Circle all of the adjectives in this sentence.

    Hank bought ripe peaches, cherry pop, and four steaks.

5. Fill in a future tense verb.

    Tomorrow Melanie _____ _____ the bus.

6. Choose the correct homophone.

   Rita picked a (flour / flower) for the table.

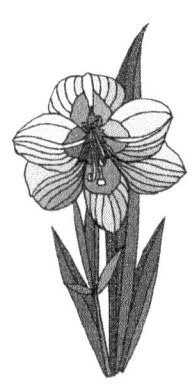

7. Underline the correct past tense verb.

   The prairie dogs have (dig / digged / dug) holes in our yard.

8. Underline the sentence that has no errors.

   Prairie dogs can be found from Canada to mexico. They are members of the squirrel family   Prairie dogs have a bark-like call.

9. Choose two antonyms.

   silly   fresh   dark   spoiled

10. Change the -y to -i and add the suffix.

    healthy + -est ➡ _____

Lesson #9

1. Choose the correct object pronoun.

   Sherry gave (I / me) a piece of cake.

2. Underline the adverb.

   The bee flew quickly to the next flower.

3. Fill in the past tense form of the verb *go*.

   The farmer _____ to the market to sell his corn.

4. Which part of the sentence is underlined?

   Linda <u>ordered Mexican food</u>.

   subject   predicate

5. Insert commas where they are needed.

   Dylan traveled to Spain France and Greece.

6. Use two editing marks to correct the sentence.

   Uncle Jack went africa.

7. Rewrite the sentence below.

   _____

   _____

   _____

8. Circle the correct verb form in the sentence.

   Dr. Lee (is / are) my veterinarian.

9. Write a compound word that means "the light of day."

   _____

10. Use the editing marks for "add end punctuation" and "make capital" to correct this sentence.

    aunt Lily left her umbrella on the bus

Lesson #10

1. What does *preorder* mean?

   _____

2. Is the underlined word a noun or a verb? _____

   Lifeguards <u>watched</u> the swimmers at the pool.

3. Make contractions.

   were not ➡ _____

   was not ➡ _____

4. Write the abbreviation for *January*.

   _____

5. Underline the subject pronoun.

   They spend too much money on candy.

Summer Solutions© Grammar & Writing   Level 3

6. In each sentence the verb is underlined. Circle the adverb that tells *when* or *where*.

   Jason <u>called</u> immediately when he got home from school.

   The little girl <u>stood</u> near her mother.

7. Underline the nouns in the sentence.

   The teacher waited for the children at the gym.

8. Draw a line through the fragment.

   Roadrunners are quick enough to catch rattlesnakes. And lizards too. Roadrunners live in the desert.

9. Add some words to the fragment to make a complete thought.

   _____

10. Write the plural of *body*.   _____

21

Lesson #11

1. Add an adjective to complete the sentence.

   We saw a _____ bear at the zoo.

2. Select the best article.

   Grandma gave me (a / an) egg with my toast.

   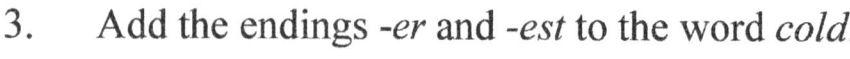

3. Add the endings -er and -est to the word *cold*.

   _____ _____

4. Underline the subject.

   My cousin went down the hill on his sled.

5. Write two sentences about going sled riding.

   _____

   _____

   _____

6. Match each word part with its meaning.

   un-   again

   re-   without

   -less   more (or one who does something)

   -er   not

7. Add *-ing* to these verbs.

   write   create   trace

   _____   _____   _____

8. Add quotation marks.

   Barb said, Please be on time for dinner.

9 – 10. Your birthday is coming up. Make a list of possible gift ideas.

   _____   _____

   _____   _____

   _____

Lesson #12

Read the paragraph and look at the words that are underlined. If there is a mistake, choose the correct way to write each underlined part. If there is no mistake, choose "no error."

(1) <u>Joshs</u> report is due on Tuesday. He is still

(2) working on the <u>Rough</u> draft. His mom will help with

(3) the typing because Josh <u>is'nt</u> very fast on the keyboard.

(4) <u>I</u> hope he gets a good grade.

1. Joshs'
   Josh's
   no error

2. rough
   ruff
   no error

3. isn't
   isnt'
   no error

4. i
   eye
   no error

5. Identify the <u>sentence type</u>.

   Do you want to play tag?   ____Question____

   We finally finished!   _____

   Bring me the hammer.   _____

6. Underline the verb.

   The giant pandas played in their cage.

7. Underline the irregular plural nouns.

   teeth   turtles

   nails   children

8. Fix this run-on. Write at least two sentences.

   My older sister likes to babysit she earns a lot of money.

   _____

   _____

9. Draw the editing mark for "take something out." _____

10. Circle two synonyms.

    huge   tiny   enormous   happy

Lesson #13

1. Sort these words into two lists: nouns and adjectives.

   table   tall   yellow   phone   barn   slippery

   Nouns ➡ _____

   Adjectives ➡ _____

2. Fill in the blank with a present tense verb.

   Sasha _____ to the bus stop.
   　　　　　(skip)

3. Underline the correct helping verb.

   Mica (has / have) read that book already.

4. Write a possessive pronoun (my, your, his, her, its, our, or their) to complete the sentence.

   Marta asked me to bring _____ tablet from the desk.

5. Underline the correct homophone.

   Our class had to (right / write) a letter to the mayor.

6. Write the abbreviation for *Friday*. _____

7 – 8. Look at the editing marks. Rewrite the sentences correctly.

I went to my cousin's wedding⊙ <u>s</u>he looked beautiful!

_____

_____

_____

9. Use an editing mark to show which word is not spelled correctly.

I was afraid to jump off the diveing board.

10. Add quotation marks.

Eugene asked, Do you know how to swim?

Lesson #14

1. Underline the correct helping verb.

   Danita (has / have) ridden the bus downtown.

2. List the possessive pronouns.

   _____ _____ _____

   _____ _____ _____ _____

3. Which word is a proper noun?

   brother   people   Harold

4. What is the object pronoun in this sentence? _____

   Marcie went with her to the library.

5. Use the editing mark for "take something out" to fix this sentence.

   She gave a talk about her trip to the Alaska.

6. Underline the subject in this sentence.

   My brother caught three frogs.

7. Add the two missing commas.

   The recipe calls for flour butter eggs, and milk.

8. Draw a line through the fragment.

   The giraffe is a mammal from Africa. The tallest of all land-living mammals. The female giraffe is a little shorter than the male giraffe.

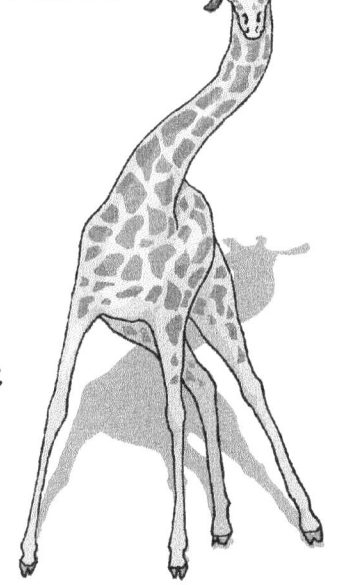

9. The prefix *re-* means "again." Fill in a word that means "wash again."

   Gina had to _____ the dishes that were still dirty.

10. Cross out the word that is misspelled. Write the misspelled word correctly.

    Look at Daniel's picure.   _____

Lesson #15

1. Underline the correct pronoun in the predicate of this sentence.

   Mom handed the plate to (I / me).

2. Fill in a conjunction to complete this sentence.

   I went to bed early, _____ I wouldn't be tired in the morning.

3. Use the prefix *un-* to write a word that means "the opposite of tied."

   _____

4. Circle two synonyms.

   choose   list   pick   close

5. Underline the adverb that tells *when* or *where*.

   Yesterday my family went to the amusement park.

6. Use the editing mark for capitalization to make three corrections in this sentence.

   Is labor day always on a monday?

7. Fill in the missing past tense verbs.

   grow, _____, had _____

   eat, _____, had _____

8. Write these contractions.

   have not ➡ _____

   has not ➡ _____

9. What kind of sentence is this?

   Look at that huge deer!   _____

10. Underline two adjectives in this sentence.

    Two bears waded in the cool water.

Lesson #16

1. Circle the conjunction.

   Tigers are the largest cats in the world, but they are also good swimmers.

2. Choose the correct verb form to complete the sentence.

   Tony (like / likes) the idea.

3. Label each noun S, for singular, or P, for plural.

   ___ boys   ___ rabbit

   ___ dishes   ___ pen

Write the verb in the <u>past tense</u> for each sentence.

4. Kiely _____ on the stranger.
   (jump)

5. Sara _____ the wet paint.
   (touch)

6. The prefix *pre-* means _____.

        not   before   again

7. Choose the sentence that has no errors.

    Jenny went to columbus for the weekend.

    She bought some new clothes for school.

8. Use editing marks to correct two errors.

    Where did You get your new bracelet

9. Write the sentence above correctly.

    _____

    _____

10. Write the words that make up the compound word below.

    quicksand ➡ _____ and _____

Lesson #17

1. List the missing steps of The Writing Process.

    1. _____Prewriting_____

    2. _____

    3. _____Revising_____

    4. _____

    5. _____Publishing_____

2. Underline the object pronoun in this sentence.

    Kelvon came with me to the doctor.

3. Underline the adverb that tells *where*.

    We searched everywhere for my watch.

4. Look at these words. Circle the conjunctions.

    new   but   happy   treehouse   and   or

5. Underline the adjectives in the list above.

6. Add a comma and quotation marks.

   The crossing guard said Wait for the light to turn red.

7. Add the suffix to make adjectives that compare.

   close + -er ➡ _____

   close + -est ➡ _____

8. Write the past tense of *worry*.

   _____

9. Write a sentence, using the verb you formed above.

   _____

   _____

10. Use the editing mark for "make capital" to correct any errors.

    Now uncle jack lives in boston.

Lesson #18

1. Add a conjunction.

   It might storm, _____ take your raincoat.

2. Underline the correct words to complete the sentence.

   (Nikki and I / Me and Nikki) took turns hitting the ball.

3. Add quotation marks.

   Abby said, How do you make stuffed peppers?

4. Underline the verb that shows "being" in the sentence.

   Kyle was late for school yesterday.

5. Use the editing mark for "check spelling" to correct two errors in this sentence.

   Heidi bought some close at the shoping center.

6. Fill in an adjective.

   Randy got a _____ puppy for Christmas.

7. Underline the adverb that tells *when*.

   Tamika often rides the bus to school.

8. Underline the correct spelling of a word that means "a pleasure to see, hear, or think about."

   butiful   beautyful   beautiful   butefull

9 – 10. This sentence is a run-on. Write it as two complete thoughts or use a conjunction to make the sentence better.

   We are learning about the planet Jupiter it is a very large planet.

   _____

   _____

   _____

   _____

Lesson #19

1. Choose the correct verb form to complete the sentence.

   Dad (fix / fixes) the snow blower when it breaks.

2. Add *-ing* to the verb. Fill in the verb to complete the sentence.

   Autumn will be _____ soon.
   (arrive)

3. Use one of these words with *news* to make a compound word.

   today   stand   picture   paper

   _____

4. Make another compound word with *news* plus a different word from question #3.

   _____

5. Circle the conjunction.

   I'm not feeling well today, so please go to the show without me.

6. Underline the correct homophone.

    Edward uses his (write / right) hand when he eats his food.

7. Add the proper end punctuation.

    Have you taken dance lessons before___

8. Edit this sentence. Use two editing marks.

    We have tickets to the Ballgame on tuesday.

9. Rewrite the sentence above correctly.

    _____

    _____

    _____

10. Fill in a future tense verb.

    Tomorrow Ty _____ _____ his favorite television program.

Summer Solutions© Grammar & Writing   Level 3

Lesson #20

1. **A simile is a comparison of two things, using *like* or *as*.** Underline the two things being compared in the sentence below.

   My mom was as happy as a child at Christmas.

2. Write the proper noun correctly.

   mr. mercer _____

3. Draw a line under the nouns that are plural.

   lions   shoe   women   turkey   classes   boat

4. Add a <u>plural possessive noun</u> to complete the sentence.

   All of the _____ books were in their book bags.
                       (boys)

5. Circle the subject pronoun.

   She has a hamster named Lefty.

6. Insert a comma and quotation marks.

   The witch cackled I'll be flying around on Halloween night.

7. Write the past tense of *draw*.

   _____

8 – 10. Write a draft about your favorite Halloween costume or your favorite Halloween experience.

_____

_____

_____

_____

Did I...

___ indent the paragraph?

___ begin each sentence with a capital letter?

___ end with proper punctuation?

___ spell words correctly?

Lesson #21

1. Draw the editing mark for "take something out." _____

2. Underline two things being compared in the simile.

    Rachel was as busy as a beaver getting ready for the party.

3. Which word in the sentence is an adverb?

    Diedre talked excitedly about her project.

4. Write the abbreviation for *February*.

    _____

5. Choose the best article to complete the sentence.

    Please take (a / an) heavy jacket with you today.

6. Draw a line through the fragment.

    I forgot my gym clothes. And my tennis shoes. I will have to sit out during gym class.

7. Choose the possessive pronouns to complete this sentence.

   Calvin walks (he / his) ferret and brushes (it / its) fur.

8. Underline the subject of the sentence.

   Our neighbor moved to Kansas.

9. Write the predicate of the sentence in #8.

   _____

10. Adjectives are words that describe. Underline the adjectives below.

    | smart | skip | bottle | helpful |
    | run | pretty | tall | truck |
    | bank | loud | boys | honest |

Lesson #22

Read the paragraph and look at the words that are underlined. Decide which part of speech each word is and write its name below.

Parts of Speech: adjective, adverb, conjunction, noun, pronoun, verb

<u>Giant</u> anteaters can live in the grasslands and the
(1)

rainforest. They <u>happily</u> eat ants <u>and</u> termites. At night,
(2) (3)

they <u>find</u> shelter in the base of a tree or a hollow <u>log</u>. If
(4) (5)

you live in the United States, <u>you</u> will probably never see a
(6)

giant anteater.

1. _____   4. _____

2. _____   5. _____

3. _____   6. _____

7. Name the sentence type.

   Clean your shoes before coming into the house.

   _____

8. **When I got in trouble at school my mom was as mad as a hornet.** What is being compared to a hornet in this simile?

   trouble   school   mom

9. Use the editing marks for "check spelling" and "add something" to fix these sentences.

   Grasshopers eat plants.   Some grasshoppers noises.

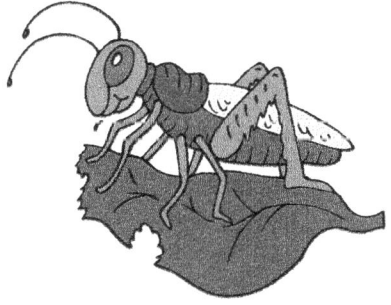

10. Rewrite the sentences from #9 correctly.

    _____

    _____

Lesson #23

1. Use the suffix *-er* to make a word that means "someone who teaches."

   _____

2. **A firefighter is a very courageous person.** Which word is a synonym for *courageous*?

   scary   happy   brave   special

3. Write the contraction for *we are*.   _____

4. Insert a comma and quotation marks.

   The bus driver yelled Get in your seats, or I will stop the bus!

5. What is the verb in this sentence?

   Marvin's horse jumped the fence.   _____

6. Draw the editing mark for "make lower case."   _____

7. Look at the next two sentences. For each sentence tell whether the underlined word is used as a noun or a verb.

   A) Please <u>wave</u> to your grandparents. _____

   B) A giant <u>wave</u> crashed into our boat. _____

8. Write a <u>possessive pronoun</u> to replace the underlined nouns.

   <u>Marcus and Leon</u> threw _____ bikes on the ground.

9 – 10. Writing Practice: Do you think a raccoon would make a good pet? Why or why not? Write a draft of at least three sentences.

_____

_____

_____

_____

_____

_____

Lesson #24

1. Which two are synonyms?

    look   race   shout   search

2. Write the words that make up the contraction in this sentence.

    Harry wasn't on the bus today.

    _____ _____

3. Make the verb in this sentence show <u>future tense</u>.

    Mr. Thomas _____ to Paris next spring.
                            (travel)

4. Underline the nouns in this sentence.

    My brother plays the guitar, the drums, and the violin.

5. Underline the predicate.

    The new library opens next week.

6. You can use similes to make your writing more interesting. Rewrite this sentence with a simile.

   My sister has a very bad temper.

   _____

   _____

7. Underline the subject pronoun in this sentence. Circle the object pronoun.

   I walked to the corner store with him.

8. Use the editing marks for "make capital" and "end punctuation" to fix this sentence.

   stephen wrote a letter to dr. brusky

9. Fill in the plural possessive noun.

   The teacher put the _____ projects in the hall.
                                (classes)

10. Write the abbreviation for *Thursday*. _____

Lesson #25

1. Insert the present tense form of the verb *study*.

   Michael _____ at least two hours a day.

2. Write a simile to describe Hank's bicycle tire.
   (Hank's bicycle tire is flat.)

   _____

   _____

3. Draw the mark for "add something."

   _____

4. Underline the correct homophone in each sentence.

   A) My teacher asked me if I (new / knew) the answer.

   B) Grandma bought me a (new / knew) coat for my birthday.

5. Write two past tenses of *do*.

   _____   _____

6 – 10. How would you go about making your favorite dessert? Use words like *first, next, then, after that,* and *finally*.

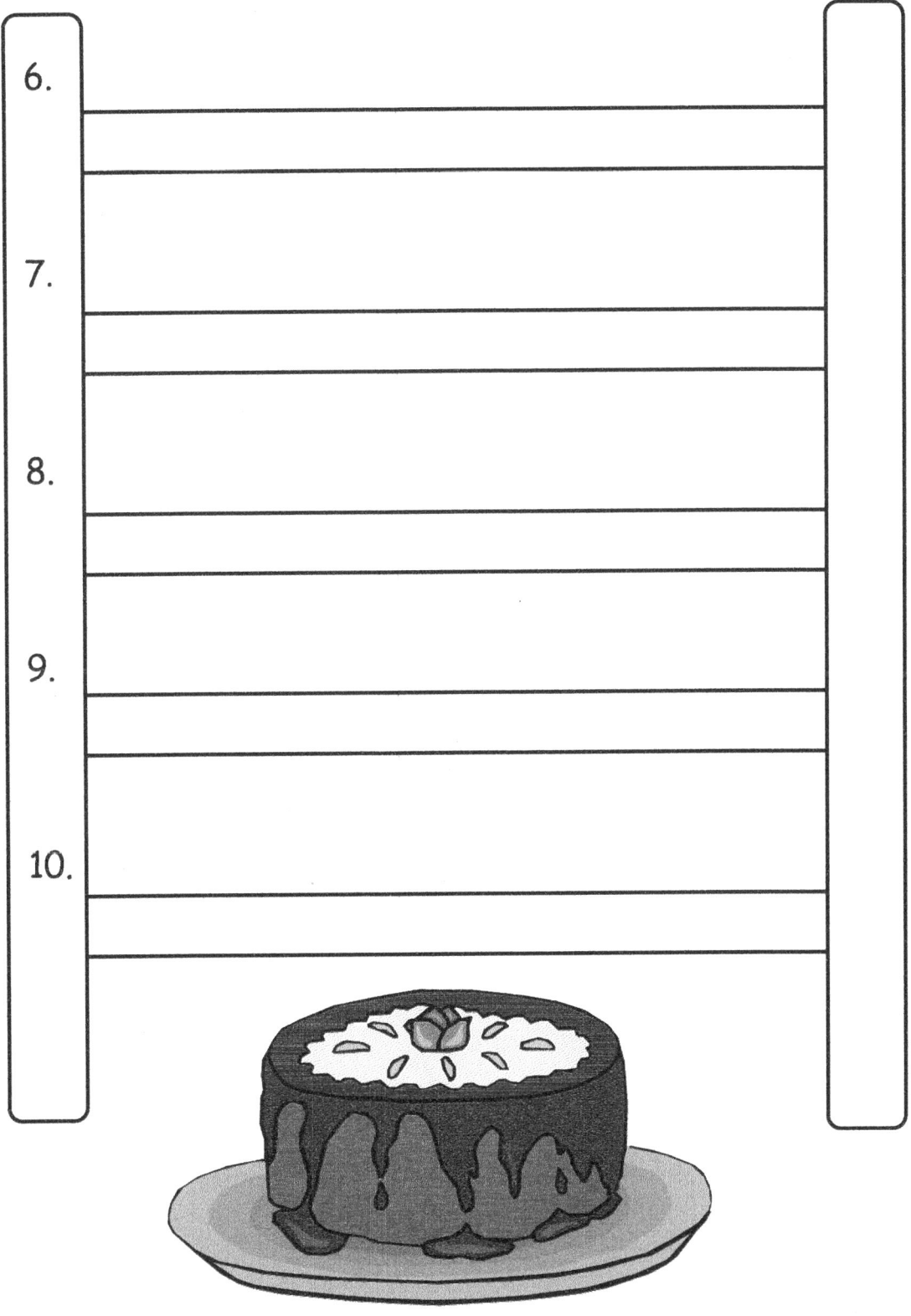

Lesson #26

1. Which word in the sentence is an adverb? _____

   Kim skied gracefully down the slope.

2. Underline two adjectives in this sentence.

   The colorful leaves landed on the soggy ground.

3. Add a comma and quotation marks to complete the sentence.

   Damond asked Can we go for a canoe ride?

4. Write the plural of *elf*.

   _____

5. Underline the sentence that has no errors.

   Tornadoes come many shapes. The most common shape is a funnel. a waterspout is a tornado over water. Tornadoes can be very dangrus.

6. A _____ names a person, place, or thing.

7. Underline the subject of the sentence.

   Coconuts are the fruit of the coconut palm tree.

8. Write the abbreviation for each word.

   December ➡ _____   mrs. ➡ _____

   Sunday ➡ _____   February ➡ _____

9 – 10. Rewrite this run-on as two complete sentences. Add any missing punctuation.

   Computers can be helpful tools you can look up information type papers and play games.

   _____

   _____

   _____

   _____

Lesson #27

1. Which word is a synonym for *tear*?

    fold   rip   bend

2. Which of these words can be added to *any* to make a compound word?

    man   body   one   person   two

3. Underline the adverb.

    Grandpa walked slowly down the stairs.

4. Underline the proper nouns in this sentence.

    Benito has lived in Chicago, Detroit, and Cleveland.

5. Use the editing marks for "make lower case" and "add something" to fix this sentence.

    She handed boy his Ticket.

6. Rewrite the sentence above with the corrections.

Summer Solutions© Grammar & Writing   Level 3

7. Add a comma and quotation marks.

   Lena screamed Go get help!

8. Draw a line through the fragment.

   A tadpole has no legs when it is first born. And a fin-like tale. Most tadpoles eat algae. Tadpoles become frogs.

9. Add some words to the fragment above to make a complete thought.

   _____

   _____

10. Circle the verb that shows "being" in this sentence.

    We are happy to see her.

55

Lesson #28

1. Circle the correct present tense verb.

   The frog (catch / catches) small insects.

2. Underline the predicate. Circle the verb.

   Our class played tag at recess.

3. Underline the singular possessive noun.

   I went to Dad's office on Monday.

4. What is the rule for making these nouns plural?

   quiz   catch   box   brush

   _____

5. Fill in the blank with a future tense verb.

   Next week Tina _____ her room.
                    (paint)

Summer Solutions© Grammar & Writing   Level 3

6. Circle the correct helping verb.

   David (have / has) given me five dollars toward the gift.

7. Fill in a possessive pronoun to complete the sentence.

   Let's put _____ toys away before dinner.

8. Use two editing marks to correct the sentence.

   Maria and brandon went to the libary.

9. Rewrite the sentence correctly.

   _____

   _____

10. Add a conjunction to make this sentence easier to read and understand.

    Our car did not start we took it to the service station.

    _____

    _____

Lesson #29

1. Write a contraction that can replace the underlined words.

   You <u>should not</u> talk on the phone during a thunderstorm.

   _____

2. Underline the correct <u>past tense</u> verb.

   The tree has (grow / grew / grown) a lot since last year.

3. Underline the <u>plural possessive</u>.

   April asked for her friends' addresses so she could send them an invitation to her party.

4. Underline the nouns.

   The children used crayons, markers, paint, and glue to make their poster.

5. Write the subject of the sentence above.

   _____

6. Underline the adverb.

Louis ran quickly toward the basket.

7. Add the suffix. Write the new word.

happy + -est ➡ _____

8. Tell what each prefix means.

un- ➡ _____ pre- ➡ _____

re- ➡ _____

9. Insert commas in the series.

Mr. Russell teaches math history spelling and science.

10. Use the word *weather* in a sentence to show its meaning.

_____

_____

Lesson #30

1. **Ashley looked as white as a ghost.** What two things are being compared in the simile?

   _____

2. Underline the correct word.

   (It's / Its) snowing in Buffalo tonight.

3. Choose the correct article.

   Please put (a / an) apple in the basket with the grapes.

4. Insert a comma and quotation marks.

   Rasheed said I believe that Mars is cooler than Earth.

5. Underline the sentence with no errors.

   The statue of liberty stands in New York Harbor. It was given to the United States by France. it is 151 feet tall. The Statue of Liberty is a symbol of fredom.

6. Write the verb that shows "being" in the sentence.

   The deer was alone in the woods.

   _____

7. Fill in an adjective.

   I had on a _____ jacket.

8. Write the abbreviation for *November*.

   _____

9. Use two editing marks to fix this sentence.

   Terrance ca'nt skate very the well.

10. Rewrite the sentence correctly.

    _____

    _____

level 3

English Grammar
& Writing Mechanics

Help Pages

Help Pages

Vocabulary:	
Sentence	a group of words that tells a complete thought
Subject	tells who or what the sentence is about
Predicate	tells what the subject does or is
Synonym	a word that means the same or almost the same as another word
Antonym	a word that means the opposite of another word
Homophone	words that sound alike but have different spellings and meanings

Parts of Speech:	
Noun	a word that names a person, place, or thing
Verb	a word that shows action or a state of being; a verb is the main word in the predicate
Pronoun	a word that takes the place of a noun
Adjective	a word that describes a noun
Article	a special type of adjective; there are only 3 (a, an, the)
Adverb	a word that describes a verb (often ends in -ly)
Conjunction	a word that connects words or phrases in a sentence (and, or, but, so)

Forms of the Verb Be:		
Present	Past	Future
am	was	will be
is	were	
are		

Help Pages

Kinds of Sentences:		
Statement	tells something	.
Question	asks something	?
Command	tells someone to do something	.
Exclamation	shows emotion	!

Editing Marks:	
Capital letter	≡
End Punctuation	⊙ ⊙ ⊙
Add Something	∧
Change to lower case	/
Take something out	ϑ
Check Spelling	sp ◯
Indent	¶

Helping Verbs:
have
has
had
will

Steps in the Writing Process:		
1.	Prewriting	getting ideas for writing
2.	Drafting	putting your ideas into writing
3.	Revising	adding or taking out to make your writing better
4.	Editing	using editing marks to correct mistakes
5.	Publishing	sharing your writing with others

Help Pages

Spelling Rules:
1. Words ending in *s, x, z, ch,* or *sh,* add *–es* to make the plural.
2. If a word has only one syllable or just one vowel, <u>double the ending consonant</u> before adding *–er* or *–est*.
3. To make compound words, usually join two words without changing the spelling of either word.
4. When adding a suffix to a word, the spelling of the word sometimes changes; the suffix does not usually change.
5. If a word ends in *–e* and you want to add a suffix that begins with a vowel, drop the *–e* before adding the suffix.
6. When a word ends in a consonant plus *y,* change the *y* to *i* and add *–es*.

Subject Pronouns:	
Singular	I, you, he, she, it
Plural	we, you, they

Object Pronouns:	
Singular	me, you, him, her, it
Plural	us, you, them

Possessive Pronouns:	
Singular	my, your, his, her, its
Plural	our, your, their

Help Pages

Verb Tenses:	
Present Tense Verbs	Most present tense verbs end in -s when the subject is singular. (The dog runs. He waits.)
Past Tense Verbs	Verbs that tell an action that has already happened usually add -ed to show past time.
Future Tense Verbs	Verbs that tell about an action that is going to happen add the helping verb *will* to show future time.

Irregular Verbs:		
Present	Past	With *has, have,* or *had*
come	came	*has, have,* or *had* come
do	did	*has, have,* or *had* done
draw	drew	*has, have,* or *had* drawn
eat	ate	*has, have,* or *had* eaten
give	gave	*has, have,* or *had* given
go	went	*has, have,* or *had* gone
grow	grew	*has, have,* or *had* grown
know	knew	*has, have,* or *had* known
run	ran	*has, have,* or *had* run
see	saw	*has, have,* or *had* seen
take	took	*has, have,* or *had* taken
write	wrote	*has, have,* or *had* written

level 3

English Grammar
& Writing Mechanics

Answers to Lessons

	Lesson #1		Lesson #2		Lesson #3
1	grown	1	fire farm	1	~~swimer~~ swimmer
2	heavy light	2	A lion tamer	2	you're wasn't
3	crashed	3	"I'm getting a new puppy today."	3	Maybe i will be in the your class next year.
4	arriving saving	4	(huge)	4	bravest
5	capital	5	lonely	5	their
6	My family is going to Brazil in June.	6	longer	6	bushes churches sticks
7	done	7	(me)	7	The nurse asked, "Do you have a cough?"
8	(huge)	8	We saw many different kinds of monkeys at the zoo.	8	a funny trick an or the olive the kittens
9	We took plates, napkins, cups, and silverware in the picnic basket.	9	play	9	(She) bakes the most delicious cakes.
10	Dr. Mason	10	four two	10	We live on a (fram). we have cows,...

	Lesson #4		Lesson #5		Lesson #6
1	warmer warmest	1	Carter asked, "Why don't we have school tomorrow?"	1	unzip unbuckle
2	slowly	2	simple difficult	2	walk
3	Feb. → February Apr. → April Dec. → December	3	stirred	3	suddenly
4	Nouns: baby, pony, bank, pen	4	Texas Lake Erie	4	a or the
5	Verbs: trot, laugh, spell	5	The sea otter	5	closest
6	Answers will vary.	6	I like to eat fries with ∧ hamburger⊙ my	6	(six) (two)
7	Answers will vary.	7	I like to eat fries with my hamburger.	7	Nov. → November Feb. → February Dec. → December
8	knew	8	have not can not is not	8	Mrs. Gomez said, "Your project is due on Tuesday."
9	their	9	Wilsons'	9	In which month ∧ valentine's Day? is
10	pete does not have a game on saturday.	10	~~Even the flowers.~~ He even ate the flowers. (Answers may vary.)	10	In which month is Valentine's Day?

	Lesson #7		Lesson #8		Lesson #9
1	Hawaii United States	1	noisily	1	me

2	Grandma	2	when: today
			     next
			     soon
			     often
			where: away
			     near
			     around
				2	quickly

3	neighbor's	3	have	3	went
4	shows	4	(ripe) (four) (cherry)	4	predicate
5	(carefully)	5	will take will ride (Answers may vary.)	5	Dylan traveled to Spain, France, and Greece.
6	Wed.	6	flower	6	Uncle Jack went to africa.
7	without meat	7	dug	7	Uncle Jack went to Africa.
8	(hid)	8	Prairie dogs have a bark-like call.	8	(is)
9-10	Answers will vary.	9	fresh spoiled	9	daylight
		10	healthiest	10	aunt Lily left her umbrella on the bus.

	Lesson #10		Lesson #11		Lesson #12
1	order before	1	(Answers will vary.) giant, black, huge ...	1	Josh's
2	verb	2	an	2	rough
3	weren't wasn't	3	colder coldest	3	isn't
4	Jan.	4	My cousin	4	no error
5	They	5	Answers will vary.	5	Exclamation Command
6	(immediately) (near)	6	un- → not re- → again -less → without -er → more	6	played
7	teacher children gym	7	writing creating tracing	7	teeth children
8	~~And lizards too.~~	8	Barb said, "Please be on time for dinner."	8	My older sister likes to babysit⊙ she earns a lot of money.
9	They can catch lizards, too. (Answers may vary.)	9-10	Answers will vary.	9	ʔ
10	bodies			10	(huge) (enormous)

	Lesson #13		Lesson #14		Lesson #15
1	<u>Nouns</u> ➡ table, barn, phone <u>Adj.</u> ➡ tall, yellow, slippery	1	<u>has</u>	1	<u>me</u>
2	skips	2	my, your, his, her, its, our, their	2	so
3	<u>has</u>	3	Harold	3	untied
4	Any of these: my, your, his her, its, our their	4	her	4	(choose) (pick)
5	<u>write</u>	5	She gave a talk about her trip to ~~the~~ Alaska.	5	<u>Yesterday</u>
6	Fri.	6	<u>My brother</u>	6	Is <u>labor</u> <u>day</u> always on a <u>monday</u>?
7-8	I went to my cousin's wedding. She looked beautiful!	7	The recipe calls for flour, butter, eggs, and milk.	7	grew had grown ate had eaten
		8	~~The tallest of all land-living mammals.~~	8	haven't hasn't
9	I was afraid to jump off the (diveing) board. sp	9	rewash	9	exclamation
10	Eugene asked, "Do you know how to swim?"	10	~~picure~~ picture	10	<u>Two</u> <u>cool</u>

74

	Lesson #16		Lesson #17		Lesson #18
1	(but)	1	2. Drafting 4. Editing	1	so
2	likes	2	me	2	Nikki and I
3	P - boys S - rabbit P - dishes S - pen	3	everywhere	3	Abby said, "How do you make stuffed peppers?"
4	jumped	4	(but) (and) (or)	4	was
5	touched	5	new happy	5	Heidi bought some (close) sp at the (shoping) sp center.
6	before	6	The crossing guard said, "Wait for the light to turn red."	6	cute, black, adorable (Answers will vary.)
7	She bought some new clothes for school.	7	closer closest	7	often
8	Where did you get your new bracelet(?)	8	worried	8	beautiful
9	Where did you get your new bracelet?	9	Answers will vary.	9	We are learning about the planet Jupiter.
10	quick sand	10	Now uncle jack lives in boston.	10	It is a very large planet.

Summer Solutions© Grammar & Writing — Level 3

	Lesson #19		Lesson #20		Lesson #21
1	fixes	1	My <u>mom</u> <u>a child at Christmas</u>	1	♂
2	arriving	2	Mr. Mercer	2	<u>Rachel</u> <u>beaver</u>
3	newspaper or	3	<u>lions</u> <u>women</u> <u>classes</u>	3	excitedly
4	newsstand	4	boys'	4	Feb.
5	(so)	5	(She)	5	a
6	<u>right</u>	6	The witch cackled, "I'll be flying around on Halloween night."	6	~~And my tennis shoes~~.
7	Have you taken dance lessons before<u>?</u>	7	drew	7	his its
8	We have tickets to the B̸allgame on <u>t</u>uesday.	8		8	<u>Our neighbor</u>
9	We have tickets to the ballgame on Tuesday.	-	Answers will vary.	9	moved to Kansas.
10	will watch / will tape (Answers may vary.)	10		10	<u>smart</u> <u>helpful</u> <u>tall</u> <u>pretty</u> <u>loud</u> <u>honest</u>

Summer Solutions© Grammar & Writing — Level 3

	Lesson #22		Lesson #23		Lesson #24
1	adjective	1	teacher	1	look search
2	adverb	2	brave	2	was not
3	conjunction	3	we're	3	will travel
4	verb	4	The bus driver yelled, "Get in your seats, or I will stop the bus!"	4	brother guitar drums violin
5	noun	5	jumped	5	opens next week.
6	pronoun	6	/	6	Answers will vary.
7	command	7	A) verb B) noun	7	I (him)
8	mom	8	their	8	stephen wrote a letter to dr. brusky⊙
9	(Grasshopers) eat sp plants. Some grasshoppers∧ make noises.	9-10	Answers will vary.	9	classes'
10	Grasshoppers eat plants. Some grasshoppers make noises.			10	Thurs.

78

Lesson #25		Lesson #26		Lesson #27	
1	studies	1	gracefully	1	rip
2	Hank's bicycle tire is as flat as a pancake. (Answers will vary.)	2	colorful soggy	2	body one
3	∧	3	Damond asked, "Can we go for a canoe ride?"	3	slowly
4	A) knew B) new	4	elves	4	Benito Detroit Chicago Cleveland
5	did have/has/had done	5	The most common shape is a funnel.	5	She handed∧boy his∧ticket. (the)
6 - 10	Answers will vary.	6	noun	6	She handed the boy his ticket.
		7	Coconuts	7	Lena screamed, "Go get help!"
		8	Dec. Mrs. Sun. Feb.	8	~~And a fin like tail.~~
		9 - 10	Computers can be helpful tools⊙ You can look up information, type papers, and play games.	9	It also has a fin-like tail. (Answers will vary.)
				10	(are)

	Lesson #28		Lesson #29		Lesson #30
1	(catches)	1	shouldn't	1	Ashley ghost
2	(played) tag at recess	2	grown	2	It's
3	Dad's	3	friends'	3	an
4	Add -es to words ending in s, x, z, ch, or sh to make the plural	4	children crayons markers paint glue poster	4	Rasheed said, "I believe that Mars is cooler than Earth."
5	will paint	5	The children	5	It was given to the United States by France.
6	(has)	6	quickly	6	was
7	your our their his her (any of these)	7	happiest	7	Answers will vary.
8	Maria and brandon went to the (libary) sp	8	un- → not pre- → before re- → again	8	Nov.
9	Maria and Brandon went to the library.	9	Mr. Russell teaches math, history, spelling, and science.	9	Terrance (ca'nt) sp skate very the well.
10	Our car did not start, so we took it to the service station.	10	We had good weather today. (Answers will vary.)	10	Terrance can't skate very well.